WILLIAMS-SONOMA

Grill

COOKBOOK

Recipes by Barbara Grunes

Photography by Joyce Oudkerk Pool

WILLIAMS-SONOMA
Founder and Vice Chairman: Chuck Williams
Book Buyer: Victoria Kalish

WELDON OWEN INC.
President: John Owen
Vice President and Publisher: Wendely Harvey
Vice President International Sales: Stuart Laurence
Chief Operating Officer: Larry Partington
Associate Publisher: Lisa Atwood
Managing Editor: Jan Newberry
Consulting Editor: Norman Kolpas
Copy Editor: Sharon Silva
Design: Kari Perin, Perin + Perin
Art Director: Diane Dempsey
Production Director: Stephanie Sherman
Production Manager: Jen Dalton
Editorial/Production Assistant: Cecily Upton
Food Stylist: Susan Massey
Prop Stylist: Carol Hacker
Photo Assistant: Arjen Kammeraad

In collaboration with Williams-Sonoma
3250 Van Ness Ave., San Francisco, CA 94109

A WELDON OWEN PRODUCTION
Copyright © 1999 Weldon Owen Inc.
814 Montgomery Street, San Francisco, CA 94133

Library of Congress
Cataloging-in-Publication Data

Grunes, Barbara
  Grill : cookbook / recipes by Barbara Grunes;
  photography by Joyce Oudkerk Pool.
     p.   cm. -- (Williams-Sonoma Cookware Series)
  Includes index.
  ISBN 1-892374-06-4
  1. Barbecue cookery. I. Pool, Joyce Oudkerk. II. Title
  III. Series.
TX840.B3G785   1999
641.5'784--dc21
                                    98-34959
                                    CIP

First Published in 1999
10 9 8 7 6 5 4 3 2 1

Manufactured by Toppan Printing Co., (H.K.) Ltd.
Printed in China

A Note on Weights and Measures:
All recipes include customary U.S. and metric measurements. Metric
conversions are based on a standard developed for these books and have
been rounded off. Actual weights may vary.

CONTENTS

Grilling is the oldest, most elemental of all cooking methods, a direct, open-air interaction between food and fire. This timeless technique has been considerably refined since the days of the crude wood fire and haunch of meat, however. Today cooks turn out sophisticated fare on specially designed grills, using easy, efficient charcoal or gas for fuel and adding flavor with marinades, spice rubs, and aromatic smoke.

Yet the appeal of grilling is far more basic than its modern paraphernalia would suggest. At any time of year, but especially in the late spring, summer, and early autumn, the simple appearance of fair weather inspires cooks every-

where to bring out their grills and start cooking outdoors. With just a little planning, an entire meal, from appetizer to dessert, can be prepared on a grill, as the 42 recipes in this book deliciously demonstrate.

In addition to main courses of meat, poultry, or seafood, you can cook all kinds of first courses, including chicken wings, skewered shrimp, oysters, and even salsas on an outdoor grill. Many vegetable accompaniments—corn on the cob, asparagus, eggplant (aubergine), leeks, portobello mushrooms—can also be easily grilled with spectacular results.

Some foods you might not ever consider cooking over an open fire are actually excellent candidates. Pizzas take on a bit of the extraordinary smoky flavor that's usually only found in a wood-burning oven. Polenta and even certain pastas can also be grilled. And don't overlook desserts. Grilled fruits, grilled cheeses, even grilled cakes make imaginative additions to an outdoor menu.

Of course, the size and scope of a grilled meal will be determined largely by the particular kind of grill you have. The recipes in this book can be prepared on grills as small as a charcoal-fueled hibachi no more than one foot (30 cm) square—the kind of unit that is ideal for toting to the beach or park for a cookout. They can also be treated to the luxury of a propane-powered grill with a cooking rack in excess of three feet (90 cm) wide. Bear in mind, however, that a small grill, with its limited cooking surface and fuel capacity, will probably limit you to cooking only a single course of a meal at one time. In contrast, the largest models,

with their outsized racks and steady supplies of gas, make it possible to grill a starter, then a main course and its side dishes together, and finally a dessert.

On these introductory pages, you will find descriptions of the basic grills available (pages 8 and 9) and instructions on how to care for them (right); information on various grilling tools and accessories (pages 10 and 11); and directions on how to choose the best fuel, start a fire, and prepare it for cooking by either direct or indirect heat (pages 12 and 13).

Once you have mastered these essentials, browse through the recipes that make up the rest of the book, select your menu, and start enjoying the pleasures of the grill.

caring for your grill

Grills are essentially low-maintenance tools, but they do require some attention. With just a little regular care, your grill will cook efficiently and cleanly for many years.

Maintenance
Brush the grate lightly with oil before you begin to cook to help keep food from sticking and make it easier to clean.

While the grill is still hot after cooking, scrape off any food particles stuck to the rack with a long-handled wire brush (below).

Don't let ashes accumulate in a charcoal grill. Clean the fire pan frequently.

After a gas grill has cooled completely, sort through its lava rocks or ceramic briquets, dislodging any bits of food that could clog the gas jets. Replace the rocks or briquets if they are heavily soiled and no longer heat efficiently.

Never line a grill or the cooking grate with any material. Grills get very hot and any foreign substance presents a risk of catching fire. Also, lining a grill with aluminum foil can prevent the necessary flow of air.

Storage
When not in use, protect your grill with a waterproof cover. If possible, store it in a roofed structure, such as a garage or garden shed.

Cooks looking to buy a grill face a wide range of choices. But strip away all the bells and whistles and you'll find that only three features truly make a difference: the type of fuel, the size of the cooking surface, and the durability of the materials.

First, determine whether you prefer a charcoal- or a gas-fueled grill. Easy-to-start, easy-to-control, and easy-to-clean gas grills are the choice of cooks who value convenience. Those who enjoy the sport of grilling as much as the results savor the intense heat and natural smoke flavor offered by charcoal grills.

The size of the grill you choose will be determined by the number of people

kettle grill

The deep, hemispherical fire pan and domed cover make this charcoal grill fuel efficient and suitable for cooking with direct or indirect heat. Vents on the cover and the fire pan offer easy control of the temperature of the fire.

gas grill

Easy-to-use gas grills allow the cook to maintain an even heat throughout long periods of grilling. Multiple controls on more sophisticated models allow separate parts of the bed to be heated for indirect-heat grilling.

for whom you usually cook, but remember that a large cooking area also means more flexibility and control. For example, sometimes a steak starts to burn before the center is done to your liking. With a large surface, you can move the meat to a cooler part of the grill and slow down the cooking.

Whatever type of grill you buy, make sure that it's built to last. A stable base that won't tip over is essential for safety. You'll also want a snug-fitting lid, and if the grill has wheels, make sure they are sturdy and wide. A cooking grate with wide, heavy rods made of a durable material will stand up to the intense heat of the fire.

portable grill

Cooks who like to grill wherever they go might consider a portable model. Lightweight and easy to carry but with a much smaller capacity than stay-at-home models, these grills are perfect for taking along to the beach, park, or campground.

hibachi

This small, portable charcoal grill is designed for direct heat cooking. It's ideal for kabobs and small cuts of meat. Bottom air vents and adjustable grate holders help regulate the heat.

Fuels and Fire Starters

For cooks using a gas grill, starting the fire is easy. Open the lid and make sure that the burner controls are turned off and that there is fuel in the tank. Then turn on the fuel valve and light the grill according to the manufacturer's instructions. Close the lid and heat the grill for 10–15 minutes before you start cooking.

Charcoal grills require more advanced fire-making skills. First, you'll need to choose a fuel. Charcoal briquets make a good fire and are easy to use, but the binding agents used in their manufacture can leave an unpleasant aftertaste in food. Natural lump charcoal makes a hotter, cleaner-burning fire.

Fire-Starting Options

The most common way to start a charcoal fire is to build a pyramid of charcoal on the grate in the fire pan, soak it with lighter fluid, and ignite it with a match. But lighter fluid (as well as presoaked briquets) can be dangerous. It contributes to air pollution and lends an unpleasant chemical taste to grilled foods. Paraffin-saturated fire starters (below) or an electric fire-starting coil are two easy-to-use alternatives.

An increasingly popular tool for starting a fire is the sheet-metal

cylinder known as a chimney starter (above): Put it on the grate, stuff crumpled newspaper in the bottom, pile the charcoal on top, and light the paper. In about 20 minutes the coals should be covered with pale gray ash. Carefully dump them onto the fire grate and you're ready to start grilling.

Direct versus Indirect Heat

Before you begin grilling, determine whether you'll need direct or indirect heat. Direct heat refers to grilling directly over the hot coals or burners. Use this cooking method for searing and for grilling foods that take less than 25 minutes to cook.

Indirect heat cooks foods using reflected heat. Use it for grilling large pieces of meat and other foods that require long cooking times. Heat circulating inside the grill cooks foods evenly, eliminating any need to turn them. It is essential to keep the grill covered when grilling with indirect heat. Every time the lid is lifted, heat escapes and the cooking time increases.

To set up a charcoal grill for indirect heat, set a drip pan (an aluminum-foil roasting pan is ideal) on the fire grate and use long-handled tongs to position the hot coals around the edge of the pan. Then put the food directly over the pan and cover the grill. For foods that require 40 minutes or more of cooking time, light a second batch of coals in another grill or other fireproof container and use them to replenish the fire as the first coals die out.

When cooking over indirect heat on a gas grill, first heat the grill using all the burners, then turn off any burners directly beneath where the food will cook and put a drip pan on the fire grate. Replace the cooking grate, put the food over the drip pan, and adjust the burners on either side of the food to equal amounts of heat.

Controlling Heat

You can regulate the heat in a charcoal grill by moving the coals with long-handled metal tongs. Push them closer together to intensify the heat or spread them out to cool the fire down. Vents serve the same purpose. Open them to feed oxygen to the fire and increase the temperature, or partially close them when you need less heat.

On a gas grill, use the dials to raise or lower the heat.

If flames flare up during grilling, don't spray them with water. Steam can cause burns, and cold water can crack the finish of a hot grill. Instead, cover the grill and close its vents. The flames will quickly die out.

direct heat

For a charcoal grill, use long-handled metal tongs to spread hot coals evenly across the area of the fire pan directly below where the food will sit. For a gas grill, heat the burners beneath the area on which you plan to cook. Set the rack 4–6 inches (10–15 cm) above the fire.

indirect heat

For a charcoal grill, use long-handled metal tongs to arrange the hot coals around the edges of the drip pan. For a gas grill, heat the grill using all the burners, then turn off any burners directly beneath where the food will cook. Set the rack 4–6 inches (10–15 cm) above the fire.

GRiLLING ACCESSORIES

Hardware stores and cookware shops offer a huge number of grilling tools and gadgets. A few are essential, some are quite useful, and others are just plain fun. Here are a handful of accessories to consider for your outdoor kitchen.

SKEWERS | A good set of skewers is essential equipment for grilling kebobs. If you've been frustrated by foods spinning on traditional round skewers, you'll appreciate flat-edged metal ones that keep items in place when you turn them on the grill. If you use wooden skewers, soak them in water for at least 15 minutes to prevent them from burning.

GRILL BASKETS | These baskets make it easier to grill delicate foods like fish that often stick to the grill. Use them, too, for grilling small foods like cherry tomatoes and asparagus that sometimes fall through the grate and into the fire. Choose one with a long, heat-proof handle to facilitate safe turning.

BASTING BRUSHES | Long-handled brushes make it easy and safe to coat food with marinades or sauces while they cook. Select a brush with long natural bristles that are well attached to a sturdy handle.

Skewers

Grill Baskets

Basting Brushes

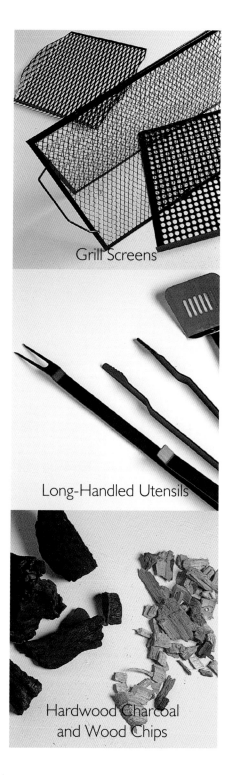

Grill Screens

Long-Handled Utensils

Hardwood Charcoal
and Wood Chips

GRILL SCREENS | An incredibly versatile grilling tool, a grill screen is ideal for cooking all those fall-through-the-cracks foods. It is great, too, for grilling fish and shellfish. Brush the screen with oil to help keep foods from sticking and let it heat for a minute. Then grill just about anything on it, including filled pastas and pizzas.

LONG-HANDLED UTENSILS | In order to move foods on a grill and still keep a safe distance from the fire, always choose grilling tools with long handles. A fork is useful for moving some foods, and no grill cook should be without a set of tongs. Use them to put food on the grill, to turn it when necessary, and to remove food when it is ready. Keep a second set of tongs for moving coals. A spatula will come in handy if you cook a lot of burgers. They are good, too, for loosening foods that are stuck to the grill.

HARDWOOD CHARCOAL AND WOOD CHIPS | The most efficient fuel for a charcoal grill is lump hardwood. Almost pure carbon, these chunks of burnt wood are easy to light and make a fire that burns hotter and cleaner than one made with charcoal briquettes. If you crave grilled food with a wood-smoked flavor, add some wood chips to the fire. In a charcoal grill, toss chips directly into the coals. In a gas grill, use a metal smoking box to hold the chips so that the fuel port doesn't get clogged.

STARTERS

Corn and Pepper Salsa

SERVES 6

This salsa travels well and can be prepared anywhere there is a grill and corn. Serve with corn bread sticks or tortilla chips.

6 slices bacon

6 ears of corn, husks and silk removed

1 large red bell pepper (capsicum), seeded and diced

4 green (spring) onions, including tender green tops, minced

Prepare a medium-hot fire for direct-heat cooking in a grill (see page 13). Position the rack 4–6 inches (10–15 cm) from the fire.

In a frying pan over medium heat, cook the bacon until crisp, about 5 minutes. Using tongs, transfer the bacon to paper towels to drain; reserve about 3 tablespoons of the drippings.

Brush the ears of corn lightly with the reserved bacon drippings, then grill, rotating the ears every 2 minutes, until slightly charred and tender, about 6 minutes. Transfer the corn to a cutting board and let cool. Then, working with 1 ear at a time, rest the ear on its stem end, and, using a sharp knife, cut down and away from you along the ear to strip off the kernels, turning the ear with each cut. Place the kernels in a bowl.

17

When all the ears are stripped, crumble the bacon and add to the bowl along with the bell pepper and green onions. Toss to mix well. Serve at room temperature. ✳

Oysters with Orange and Cognac

SERVES 6

If you've never grilled oysters before, you're in for a treat. Because they steam in their own juices, with nothing to dilute their flavor, they have an intense taste of the sea. Just be sure to grab the oysters off the grill as soon as their shells pop open. The point is simply to warm them slightly, not to cook them all the way through.

FOR THE ORANGE-COGNAC BUTTER

¾ cup (6 oz/185 g) unsalted butter, at room temperature, cut into pieces

1 tablespoon grated orange zest

3 tablespoons cognac or other brandy

3 tablespoons ground almonds

24 oysters in the shell, well scrubbed

18

Prepare a hot fire for direct-heat cooking in a covered grill (see page 13). Position the rack 4–6 inches (10–15 cm) from the fire.

To make the butter, in a food processor, combine the butter, orange zest, cognac, and almonds. Process until blended. Alternatively, combine the ingredients in a bowl and beat together with a wooden spoon. (The butter can be made up to 1 day in advance; cover and refrigerate, then bring to room temperature before serving.)

Arrange the oysters, cupped shell down, on the grill rack. Cover, open the vents, and grill just until the oysters pop open, 3–6 minutes; the timing will depend on their size.

Using long-handled tongs, transfer the oysters to a serving platter, and remove and discard the top shells, being careful not to spill the liquid. Spoon a dab of butter on top of each oyster and serve. ✷

Thai Shrimp on Lemongrass Skewers

SERVES 6

A thin, firm stalk of lemongrass makes an aromatic skewer for shrimp. Serve these shrimp with a cucumber salad seasoned with rice vinegar and fresh cilantro (fresh coriander).

6 thin stalks fresh lemongrass

FOR THE THAI BRUSHING SAUCE

¼ cup (2 fl oz/60 ml) lime juice

1 tablespoon Asian fish sauce

¼ cup (⅓ oz/10 g) chopped fresh mint

4 cloves garlic, minced

¼ teaspoon salt

¼ teaspoon red pepper flakes

2 lb (1 kg) jumbo shrimp (prawns), peeled and deveined

3 green (spring) onions, white part only, trimmed to 2-inch (5-cm) lengths

Using a small, sharp knife, shape the root end of each lemongrass stalk into a point. Soak the lemongrass stalks in water to cover for about 30 minutes. Drain.

To make the brushing sauce, combine the lime juice, fish sauce, mint, garlic, salt, and red pepper flakes. Taste and adjust the seasonings.

Meanwhile, prepare a medium-hot fire for direct-heat cooking in a covered grill (see page 13). Position the rack 4–6 inches (10–15 cm) from the fire.

Carefully thread the shrimp and green onions onto the stalks and brush the shrimp with the sauce. Place on the grill, cover, open the vents, and grill, turning once, until the shrimp are cooked through, 6–8 minutes.

Transfer to individual plates and serve hot. ✳

Buffalo Chicken Wings

SERVES 6

⅓ cup (3 fl oz/80 ml) vegetable oil

1 small clove garlic, minced

½ teaspoon cayenne pepper

2 tablespoons red wine vinegar

½ teaspoon Tabasco or other hot-pepper sauce,
or to taste

24 chicken wings, about 2 lb (1 kg) total weight

FOR THE BLUE CHEESE DRESSING

1 cup (8 fl oz/250 ml) mayonnaise

½ cup (4 fl oz/125 ml) sour cream

1 small yellow onion, minced

3 cloves garlic, minced

2 tablespoons red wine vinegar

¼ cup (⅓ oz/10 g) minced fresh parsley

½ cup (2½ oz/75 g) crumbled blue cheese

6 large celery stalks, trimmed and cut into
3-inch (7.5-cm) lengths

20

Prepare a medium-hot fire for direct-heat cooking in a grill (see page 13). Position the rack 4–6 inches (10–15 cm) from the fire.

In a bowl, stir together the vegetable oil, garlic, cayenne, vinegar, and hot-pepper sauce. Cut each wing at the joint to make 2 pieces, add to the bowl, and toss gently to coat evenly.

Arrange the wings on an oiled grill screen and grill, turning once, until cooked through, about 6 minutes on each side.

Meanwhile, make the dressing: Stir together the mayonnaise, sour cream, onion, garlic, vinegar, parsley, and blue cheese.

Transfer the wings to serving plates and serve with the celery and the blue cheese dressing. ✶

Grilled Vegetables with Two Dipping Sauces

SERVES 6–8

Here, grilled vegetables are served with a pair of full-flavored dipping sauces. You can substitute your favorite vegetables for the ones listed below. For easy entertaining, the sauces can be prepared the day before serving.

FOR THE TAPENADE

¾ cup (4 oz/125 g) pitted Kalamata olives

4 or 5 anchovy fillets in olive oil

1 clove garlic, chopped

2 tablespoons capers

1 teaspoon chopped fresh basil

2 tablespoons chopped fresh flat-leaf (Italian) parsley

1 tablespoon lemon juice

1 slice day-old white bread, torn into small pieces

1 cup (8 fl oz/250 ml) olive oil

FOR THE TOMATO SALSA

1 yellow onion, minced

½ cup (¾ oz/20 g) chopped fresh cilantro
(fresh coriander)

2 tomatoes, finely chopped

1 small red bell pepper (capsicum), seeded and chopped

salt and ground pepper to taste

1 lb (500 g) cherry tomatoes, stems removed

⅓ lb (155 g) snow peas (mangetouts), trimmed

1 zucchini (courgette), cut into slices ¼ inch (6 mm) thick

1 red (Spanish) onion, cut into quarters through the stem end
and layers separated

olive oil for brushing

To make the tapenade, in a food processor or a blender, combine the olives, anchovies, garlic, capers, basil, parsley, lemon juice, and bread. Process until smooth. With the motor running, gradually add the olive oil and process until a thick paste forms. Spoon into a bowl, cover, and refrigerate until serving. You should have about 1¼ cups (10 oz/315 g).

To make the salsa, in a small bowl, toss together the onion, cilantro, tomatoes, and bell pepper. Season with salt and pepper. Cover and refrigerate. Toss again just before serving. You should have about 2 cups (12 oz/375 g).

Soak about 16 wooden skewers in water to cover for at least 30 minutes, then drain. Meanwhile, prepare a medium-hot fire for direct-heat cooking in a grill (see page 13). Position the rack 4–6 inches (10–15 cm) from the fire.

Thread the vegetables on the skewers, dividing them evenly. Lightly brush the vegetables with olive oil and place on a grill screen. Grill, turning once, until heated through and beginning to brown, 1–2 minutes on each side.

Transfer the vegetables to a serving platter. Serve warm with the tapenade and the salsa. ✳

23

VEGETABLES AND SIDES

Grilled Portobello Mushrooms on Salad Greens

SERVES 6

FOR THE RED WINE MARINADE

½ cup (4 fl oz/125 ml) dry red wine

½ cup (4 fl oz/125 ml) vegetable oil

½ cup (4 fl oz/125 ml) fresh orange juice

1 tablespoon fresh basil

6 large fresh portobello mushrooms, stemmed

FOR THE MUSTARD VINAIGRETTE

1 tablespoon Dijon mustard

3 tablespoons red wine vinegar

½ teaspoon salt

¼ teaspoon pepper

½ cup (4 fl oz/125 ml) extra-virgin olive oil

8 cups (8 oz/250 g) torn assorted salad greens

27

To make the marinade, in a small bowl, stir together the wine, oil, orange juice, and basil. Divide between 2 large lock-top plastic bags. Put 3 mushrooms in each bag, seal, and turn several times to coat evenly. Let stand at room temperature for 1 hour.

To make the vinaigrette, in a large bowl, whisk together the mustard, vinegar, salt, and pepper. Slowly whisk in the olive oil. Set aside.

Prepare a medium-hot fire for direct-heat cooking in a covered grill (see page 13). Position the rack 4–6 inches (10–15 cm) from the fire.

Place the mushrooms on the grill rack, cover, open the vents, and grill, turning once, until moist on the underside and just firm to the touch on the top, 3–4 minutes on each side. Remove from the grill.

Add the greens to the bowl with the vinaigrette and toss well. Divide among individual plates. Slice the mushrooms into slices about ¼ inch (6 mm) thick, divide among the salads, and serve. ✳

Grilled Eggplant Salad

SERVES 6

Sprinkle this smoky eggplant salad with chopped fresh parsley and serve as a first course or side dish. Add ½ cup (2 oz/60 g) toasted pine nuts with the olives, if desired. Grilled slices of coarse country bread go well with this dish.

2 medium-large eggplants (aubergines), peeled and cut into slices ¼ inch (6 mm) thick

3 yellow onions, cut into rounds ½ inch (12 mm) thick

olive oil for brushing

4 cloves garlic, minced

1 cup (4 oz/125 g) diced celery

2 cups (12 oz/375 g) seeded and chopped tomatoes

1 cup (5 oz/155 g) oil-cured black olives, pitted

¼ cup (2 fl oz/60 ml) olive oil

2 tablespoons red wine vinegar

salt and ground pepper to taste

6 large red-leaf lettuce leaves

Prepare a medium-hot fire for direct-heat cooking in a covered grill (see page 13). Position the rack 4–6 inches (10–15 cm) from the fire.

Brush the eggplant and onion slices on both sides with olive oil. Place on an oiled grill screen, cover, open the vents, and grill, turning as necessary, until the eggplants are soft, 12–15 minutes, and the onions are slightly charred, about 5 minutes. Transfer to a platter and let cool.

In a food processor, combine the eggplants, onions, and garlic and pulse to chop coarsely. Transfer to a bowl and stir in the celery, tomatoes, olives, ¼ cup (2 fl/60 ml) olive oil, vinegar, salt, and pepper. Line 6 individual serving plates with the lettuce leaves, mound the salad on top, dividing evenly, and serve. ✳

Crisp Tofu with Oyster Sauce

SERVES 6

Oyster sauce, a thick, concentrated paste made from oysters, brine, and soy sauce, is available in well-stocked food stores and in Asian markets. Serve the tofu and vegetables over brown or white rice and sprinkle with pickled ginger.

1 package (12 oz/375 g) firm tofu, drained and cut into slices ¾ inch (2 cm) thick

3 tablespoons oyster sauce

6 green (spring) onions, trimmed but left whole

¼ lb (125 g) snow peas (mangetouts), trimmed

2 green bell peppers (capsicums), seeded and cut lengthwise into strips ½ inch (12 mm) wide

vegetable oil or canola oil for brushing

Prepare a medium-hot fire for direct-heat cooking in a grill (see page 13). Position the rack 4–6 inches (10–15 cm) from the fire.

Brush the tofu slices on both sides with the oyster sauce. Brush the green onions, snow peas, and bell peppers with the oil. Place the tofu and vegetables on an oiled grill screen and grill, turning the tofu once and the vegetables as necessary, until the tofu is crisp and heated through and the peppers, onions, and snow peas are tender and slightly charred, about 6 minutes for the vegetables and about 10 minutes for the tofu.

Transfer to a warmed platter and serve hot. ✳

Grilled Corn
with Seasoned Butters

SERVES 6

*Fresh corn still in the husk takes wonderfully to grilling.
Serve it with one or all of the seasoned butters here and a platter
full of ribs hot off the grill (page 74).*

6 ears of corn

seasoned butter (see below)

Prepare a medium-hot fire for direct-heat cooking on a covered grill (see page 13). Position the rack 4–6 inches (10–15 cm) from the fire.

Working with 1 ear at a time, carefully pull back the husks but leave them attached. Remove and discard the silk, then replace the husks around the ear. Soak the ears in cold water to cover for at least 20 minutes and then drain.

Carefully pull back the husks from each ear and spread the seasoned butter evenly over the kernels. Replace the husks.

Place the corn on the grill rack, cover, open the vents, and grill until the husks are browned and the kernels are tender, about 15 minutes. Transfer the corn to individual plates or a platter and serve hot. ✳

FOR THE PECAN BUTTER

⅓ cup (3 oz/90 g) unsalted butter, at room temperature

⅓ cup (1½ oz/45 g) ground pecans

To make the pecan butter, in a small bowl, using a fork or a wooden spoon, beat the butter until soft. Mix in the pecans to distribute evenly. Refrigerate if not using immediately.

FOR THE LIME BUTTER

⅓ cup (3 oz/90 g) butter, at room temperature

1 tablespoon grated lime zest

1 tablespoon lime juice

To make the lime butter, in a small bowl, using a fork or a wooden spoon, beat the butter until soft. Mix in the lime zest and juice to distribute evenly. Refrigerate if not using immediately.

FOR THE CHILI BUTTER

⅓ cup (3 oz/90 g) butter, at room temperature

2 tablespoons chili powder

1 teaspoon cumin seeds

To make the chili butter, in a small bowl, using a fork or a wooden spoon, beat the butter until soft. Mix in the chili powder and cumin seeds to distribute evenly. Refrigerate if not using immediately.

FOR THE ITALIAN HERB BUTTER

⅓ cup (3 oz/90 g) unsalted butter, at room temperature

2 teaspoons minced fresh basil

2 teaspoons minced fresh oregano

To make the Italian herb butter, in a small bowl, using a fork or a wooden spoon, beat the butter until soft. Mix in the basil and oregano to distribute evenly. Refrigerate if not using immediately.

Grilled Asparagus

SERVES 6

*If the asparagus spears are thick, peel the stalks with
a vegetable peeler, starting about 2 inches (5 cm) below the tips.
White asparagus are also good grilled.*

1½ lb (750 g) asparagus spears

⅓ cup (3 fl oz/80 ml) olive oil

3 tablespoons freshly grated Parmesan cheese

1 tablespoon grated lemon zest

salt and ground pepper to taste

Prepare a medium-hot fire for direct-heat cooking in a grill (see page 13). Position the rack 4–6 inches (10–15 cm) from the fire.

Snap off the tough ends from the asparagus spears. Brush the spears with about half of the olive oil and place them directly on the grill rack or on an oiled grill screen. Grill, turning once, until the asparagus are slightly charred, about 5 minutes on each side.

Transfer to a serving platter and sprinkle with the remaining olive oil, cheese, lemon zest, salt, and pepper. Serve hot. ✳

32

Grilled Leeks and Mushrooms

SERVES 6

For a subtle aromatic effect, soak ½ cup (1 oz/30 g) dried oregano in water for 5 minutes, drain well, and then sprinkle the herb over the hot coals.

6 leeks, including 2 inches (5 cm) of the tender greens, halved lengthwise

1 lb (500 g) fresh brown, white, or oyster mushrooms, brushed clean and trimmed

olive oil for brushing and sprinkling

balsamic vinegar for brushing and sprinkling

¼ cup (⅓ oz/10 g) chopped fresh oregano

½ teaspoon salt

¼ teaspoon ground pepper

1 tablespoon grated orange zest

33

Prepare a medium-hot fire for direct-heat cooking in a grill (see page 13). Position the rack 4–6 inches (10–15 cm) from the fire.

Brush the leeks and the mushrooms with the olive oil and vinegar. Sprinkle with the oregano, salt, and pepper.

Arrange the vegetables on an oiled grill screen and grill, turning as necessary, until tender, about 6 minutes for the mushrooms and 10 minutes for the leeks.

Transfer the leeks and mushrooms to a platter. Drizzle with a little more oil and vinegar and sprinkle with the orange zest. Serve warm. ✳

PIZZA AND PASTA

Double Tomato Pizza

SERVES 4–6

*For a crisper crust, grill the dough without any toppings for
a minute or two, turn it over, add the toppings, and continue to cook.*

1 recipe (10 oz/315 g) pizza dough (page 42)

olive oil for brushing and drizzling

3 large red or yellow tomatoes, sliced

3 plum (Roma) tomatoes, chopped

½ lb (250 g) fresh goat cheese, crumbled

2 tablespoons chopped garlic

2 tablespoons chopped fresh rosemary

salt and ground pepper to taste

Prepare the pizza dough as directed.

Prepare a medium-hot fire for direct-heat cooking in a covered grill
(see page 13). Position the rack 4–6 inches (10–15 cm) from the fire.
Place a pizza stone on the grill rack.

On a lightly floured work surface, roll out the dough into a round
about 12 inches (30 cm) in diameter.

Brush the surface of the dough with olive oil and then arrange the
tomato slices on top. Scatter the chopped tomatoes, goat cheese, and
garlic over the tomato slices. Sprinkle with the rosemary, salt, and
pepper and drizzle lightly with the olive oil.

Place the pizza directly on the hot pizza stone. Cover, open the vents,
and grill, rotating the crust 180 degrees after about 4 minutes, until
it is lightly browned, 8–10 minutes.

Transfer the pizza to a cutting board and cut into wedges. Serve
immediately on warmed individual plates. ✶

Grilled Ravioli with Spinach and Two Cheeses

SERVES 6

Briefly grilling cooked ravioli gives it a deliciously crisp, brown exterior that transforms the familiar pasta into a surprisingly different hors d'oeuvre.

FOR THE PASTA DOUGH

2¼ cups (11½ oz/360 g) all-purpose (plain) flour

¼ teaspoon salt

3 eggs

FOR THE TWO-CHEESE FILLING

3 cups (3 oz/90 g) spinach leaves, stems removed and chopped

1 cup (8 oz/250 g) ricotta cheese

½ cup (2 oz/60 g) shredded mozzarella cheese

1 tablespoon chopped fresh basil

salt and ground pepper to taste

olive oil for brushing

½ cup (2 oz/60 g) grated romano cheese

2 tablespoons chopped fresh basil (optional)

To make the dough, in a food processor, combine the flour and salt. Pulse briefly to combine. With the motor running, add the eggs, one at a time, and process until mixed. The dough will be very soft. Transfer the dough to a lightly floured work surface and knead for a few minutes until smooth. Divide the dough into 4 equal portions and flatten each into a disk.

If using a pasta machine, set the rollers at the widest setting, dust a dough disk with flour, and feed it through the rollers. Fold in quarters, turn 90 degrees, and feed through again. Repeat, dusting the dough with flour as needed and decreasing the roller opening one notch each time as the dough becomes smoother and silkier, until the dough is very thin. Set aside on a floured work surface. Repeat with the remaining dough portions. Alternatively, dust a work surface lightly with flour. Working with 1 piece of dough at a time, flatten each disk with your hand and, using a rolling pin, roll the dough as thinly as possible. Lightly sprinkle a dish towel with flour and leave the pasta to dry on it while you make the filling.

To make the filling, place the spinach in a saucepan with the rinsing water clinging to the leaves and place over medium heat. Cook until wilted, 2–3 minutes, then drain well and squeeze out the excess moisture with your hands. Put the spinach in a bowl and add the ricotta cheese, mozzarella cheese, basil, salt, and pepper. Mix well.

Using a pastry brush, lightly coat 1 pasta sheet with water. Using a teaspoon, place mounds of the filling on the pasta sheet, spacing them about 3 inches (7.5 cm) apart. Place a second sheet of dough on top. Press down along the edges and around the mounds. Using a pastry wheel with a fluted edge, cut between the mounds into 2½-inch (6-cm) squares. Repeat with the remaining pasta sheets and filling.

Prepare a medium-hot fire for direct-heat cooking in a grill (see page 13). Position the rack 4–6 inches (10–15 cm) from the fire.

Bring a large pot three-fourths full of salted water to a boil. Slide in the ravioli and cook until they rise to the surface and are tender, about 2 minutes. Drain well.

Brush the ravioli with olive oil, place them on an oiled grill screen, and grill, turning once, until golden brown and crisp, about 2 minutes on each side.

Transfer the ravioli to a serving platter and sprinkle with the romano cheese. Garnish with the basil, if desired, and serve hot. ✳

Grilled Polenta Wedges

SERVES 6

*The polenta can be made on the stove top a day ahead and
then grilled just before serving. Adding the cornmeal to cold water
eliminates the lumps that sometimes form. If desired, sprinkle
a handful of toasted pine nuts or chopped walnuts over the surface of
the polenta as soon as it is poured into the baking pan.*

olive oil for brushing

4 cups (32 fl oz/1 l) water

1⅓ cups (7 oz/220 g) white or yellow cornmeal

2 tablespoons chopped fresh basil

2 tablespoons chopped fresh tarragon

2 teaspoons unsalted butter, at room temperature

½ teaspoon salt

¼ cup (2 oz/60 g) drained and chopped oil-packed
sun-dried tomatoes (optional)

40

Oil a 9-inch (23-cm) round baking pan with olive oil.

Pour the water into a large saucepan. Whisk in the cornmeal, basil,
tarragon, butter, salt, and the sun-dried tomatoes, if using. Bring
to a boil over medium-high heat, whisking often. Reduce the heat
to a simmer and continue whisking until the mixture is thick and
smooth and pulls away from the sides of the pan, about 20 minutes.
Pour the polenta into the prepared pan, cover loosely with plastic
wrap, and refrigerate until firm, about 30 minutes.

Prepare a medium-hot fire for direct-heat cooking in a grill (see
page 13). Position the rack 4–6 inches (10–15 cm) from the fire.

Cut the polenta into 6 wedges. Lightly brush the polenta wedges on
both sides with olive oil and place on an oiled grill screen. Grill,
turning once, until heated through and beginning to color, about
3 minutes on each side.

Transfer the polenta wedges to a warmed platter and serve. ✳

Grilled Ratatouille Pizza

SERVES 6

FOR THE PIZZA DOUGH

1 teaspoon sugar

scant 1 cup (8 fl oz/250 ml) warm water

1 package (2½ teaspoons) active dry yeast

2¾ cups (14 oz/440 g) all-purpose (plain) flour

½ teaspoon salt

2 tablespoons olive oil

FOR THE TOPPING

1 large eggplant (aubergine), peeled and cut
into slices ½ inch (12 mm) thick

1 zucchini (courgette), cut into slices ½ inch (12 mm) thick

1 large yellow onion, cut into slices ½ inch (12 mm) thick

2 large tomatoes, cut into slices ½ inch (12 mm) thick

olive oil for brushing and drizzling

2 tablespoons chopped fresh oregano

½ teaspoon salt

¼ teaspoon ground pepper

¼ cup (1 oz/30 g) grated Parmesan
or pecorino romano cheese

42

To make the dough, in a small bowl, dissolve the sugar in the warm water. Sprinkle the yeast over the top and let stand until foamy, about 5 minutes.

In a food processor, combine the flour and salt and pulse briefly to combine. Add the olive oil and the yeast mixture and process until a soft, slightly sticky dough forms, about 10 seconds. (Alternatively, combine the ingredients in the bowl and stir with a wooden spoon until combined.)

Turn out the dough onto a lightly floured work surface and knead until smooth, about 5 minutes. If the dough is too sticky, work in more flour, a tablespoon at a time, until smooth. Gather the dough into a ball, place in a bowl, cover with a kitchen towel, and let rise in a warm place until doubled in bulk, 45–60 minutes.

Meanwhile, prepare a medium-hot fire for direct-heat cooking in a covered grill (see page 13). Position the rack 4–6 inches (10–15 cm) from the fire. Place a pizza stone on the grill rack.

To make the topping, brush the eggplant, zucchini, onion, and tomato slices generously with oil, set on a grill screen, and place the screen on the grill rack. Grill, turning once, until tender, about 2 minutes on each side for the tomatoes, about 4 minutes on each side for the zucchini, about 5 minutes on each side for the onion, and up to 7 minutes on each side for the eggplant. Transfer the vegetables to a platter. Separate the onion slices into rings.

Punch down the dough and let stand for 5 minutes. Turn out onto the floured work surface and knead for a few minutes until smooth. Roll out the dough into a round about 12 inches (30 cm) in diameter.

Brush the top surface of the dough with olive oil and place directly on the hot pizza stone. Arrange the eggplant slices over the dough and top with the zucchini, onion, and tomatoes. Sprinkle with the oregano, salt, and pepper, and drizzle lightly with olive oil.

43

Cover, open the vents, and grill, rotating once, until the crust is golden, 8–10 minutes. (The crust may take a bit longer to cook on a gas grill.) Watch carefully, as the crust may burn if the coals are too hot.

Transfer the pizza to a serving platter, sprinkle with the cheese, and cut into serving pieces. Serve hot. ✳

Grilled Vegetable Pasta

SERVES 6

Use rosemary branches as skewers for grilling: Strip most of the leaves from the stems and soak in water for about 30 minutes before using.

FOR THE DRESSING

⅓ cup (3 fl oz/80 ml) olive oil

⅓ cup (3 fl oz/80 ml) rice wine vinegar

2 cloves garlic, minced

1 tablespoon peeled and grated fresh ginger

ground pepper to taste

3 carrots, peeled and sliced ¼ inch (6 mm) thick

2 Asian (slender) eggplants (aubergines), trimmed and cut on the diagonal into slices ½ inch (12 mm) thick

1 red bell pepper (capsicum), seeded and cut crosswise into slices ½ inch (12 mm) thick

2 yellow summer squashes, sliced ½ inch (12 mm) thick

olive oil for brushing

¾ lb (375 g) penne

45

Prepare a medium-hot fire for direct-heat cooking in a grill (see page 13). Position the rack 4–6 inches (10–15 cm) from the fire.

To make the dressing, in a large bowl, whisk together the olive oil, vinegar, garlic, ginger, and pepper. Set aside.

Bring a saucepan three-fourths full of salted water to a boil. Add the carrots and parboil for 5 minutes. Drain and pat dry. Thread the carrots, eggplant, bell pepper, and squash slices onto 6 skewers, dividing evenly. Brush with the oil. Grill, turning as necessary, until tender, about 15 minutes.

Meanwhile, bring a large saucepan three-fourths full of salted water to a boil. Add the penne, stir well, and cook until firm yet tender to the bite, about 10 minutes or according to the package directions. Drain, transfer to the bowl with the dressing, and toss to coat. Serve in warmed bowls, topped with the grilled vegetable skewers. ✴

SEAFOOD, POULTRY, AND MEAT

Grilled Tuna Niçoise

SERVES 6

The slender French green beans known as haricots verts are best for this salad, but other green beans are fine. Serve with plenty of crusty French bread.

FOR THE DRESSING

⅓ cup (3 fl oz/80 ml) lemon juice

2 cloves garlic, mashed

1½ teaspoons Dijon mustard

½ teaspoon salt

½ teaspoon sugar

¼ teaspoon ground pepper

⅓ cup (3 fl oz/80 ml) olive oil

48

6 small red potatoes, about 1¼ lb (625 g) total weight, unpeeled

1 lb (500 g) green beans, trimmed

1 head butter (Boston) lettuce, leaves separated

3 large tomatoes, sliced

½ lb (250 g) Niçoise olives

1 red (Spanish) onion, sliced

2 jars (2 oz/60 g each) anchovy fillets in olive oil, drained

1½ lb (750 g) tuna steaks, about ¾ inch (2 cm) thick

olive oil for brushing

To make the dressing, in a small bowl, whisk together the lemon juice, garlic, mustard, salt, sugar, and pepper. Slowly whisk in the olive oil. Set aside.

In a saucepan, combine the potatoes with salted water to cover. Bring to a boil and cook until tender, about 20 minutes. With a slotted spoon, remove the potatoes; let cool, then slice ½ inch (12 mm) thick. Set aside. Add the green beans to the boiling water and cook until barely tender, about 10 minutes. Drain well and let cool.

Divide the lettuce leaves among individual plates, forming a bed on each plate. Decoratively set the tomatoes, potatoes, and green beans on the perimeter of each lettuce bed, dividing evenly. Divide the olives, onion slices, and anchovies evenly among the salads.

Prepare a medium-hot fire for direct-heat cooking in a grill (see page 13). Position the rack 4–6 inches (10–15 cm) from the fire.

Brush the tuna with olive oil, place on an oiled grill screen, cover, open the vents, and grill for 3–4 minutes. Brush again with oil, then turn and continue to grill until opaque throughout, 3–4 minutes longer; the timing will depend upon the thickness of the fish.

Transfer the tuna to a plate, break into irregular chunks with a fork, and arrange in the center of each salad, dividing evenly. Drizzle all the ingredients with the dressing and serve. ✳

Halibut Veracruz Style

SERVES 6

If halibut is unavailable, substitute red snapper. Serve with tortillas wrapped in aluminum foil and heated on the grill.

3 boiling potatoes, about 1 lb (500 g) total weight, unpeeled

5 halibut steaks, each 6–7 oz (185–220 g) and ¾ inch (2 cm) thick

3 yellow onions, cut into slices ½ inch (12 mm) thick

6 tomatoes, cut into quarters

olive oil for brushing

salt and ground pepper to taste

1 tablespoon chili powder

¾ cup (4 oz/125 g) stuffed green olives

3 limes, cut into wedges

In a saucepan, combine the potatoes with salted water to cover and bring to a boil. Cook until tender, about 20 minutes. Drain, let cool, and cut into slices ½ inch (12 mm) thick.

Prepare a medium-hot fire for direct-heat cooking in a grill (see page 13). Position the rack 4–6 inches (10–15 cm) from the fire.

Brush the fish steaks, onions, tomatoes, and potatoes on both sides with olive oil and season with salt and pepper. Sprinkle the fish on both sides with the chili powder. Place the fish and vegetables on a grill screen on the grill rack and grill until the fish is lightly browned, about 2 minutes. Turn the fish over and continue to cook until it is opaque throughout, 5–10 minutes longer. Cook the vegetables, turning as necessary, until softened and warm throughout, about 5 minutes for the tomatoes and 10 minutes for the potatoes and onions.

Transfer the fish steaks to a warmed platter. Scatter the vegetables and the green olives over the top and serve with lime wedges. ✳

Provençal-Style Mussels with Garlic Bruschetta

If your fishmonger can't supply you with seaweed, cook the mussels directly on a grill screen or rack. For an aromatic accent, soak a small handful of herbes de Provence in water for 5 minutes, drain, and scatter the herbs over the hot coals just before covering the grill.

FOR THE PROVENÇAL SAUCE

2 tablespoons olive oil

2 large shallots, minced

3 cloves garlic, minced

4 large tomatoes, peeled, seeded, and chopped

½ cup (2½ oz/75 g) peeled and grated carrot

1 teaspoon dried herbes de Provence

salt and ground pepper to taste

12 large cloves garlic, unpeeled

seaweed to cover grill screen (optional)

3 lb (1.5 kg) mussels

olive oil for brushing

6 slices French bread, cut on the diagonal

Prepare a hot fire for direct-heat cooking in a covered grill (see page 13). Position the rack 4–6 inches (10–15 cm) from the fire.

To make the sauce, in a saucepan over medium heat, warm the olive oil. Add the shallots and garlic and sauté, stirring occasionally, until soft, about 5 minutes. Stir in the tomatoes, carrot, herbes de Provence, salt, and pepper. Simmer until the tomatoes are soft, 5–8 minutes. Taste and adjust the seasonings. Reheat just before serving.

Place the whole garlic cloves on a piece of aluminum foil and wrap to enclose. Put the wrapped garlic on the grill rack and cook until soft, about 10 minutes (squeeze a clove to test). Transfer to a dish, unwrap, and discard the foil.

Spread the seaweed, if using, on a grill screen. Arrange the mussels on top in a single layer, discarding any mussels that do not close to the touch. Set the screen on the grill rack, cover, open the vents, and grill until the mussels open, 4–5 minutes, discarding any that have not opened. Using tongs, transfer the mussels to a heatproof platter.

Brush the bread on both sides with the olive oil and grill, turning once, until toasted, 3–5 minutes on each side.

Bring the mussels, the garlic cloves, hot Provençal sauce, and toasted bread to the table. Serve hot. Have your guests squeeze the garlic cloves from their skins onto the hot bread for spreading. ✳

53

Swordfish Drizzled with Balsamic-Butter Sauce

SERVES 6

Swordfish is a particularly good fish for grilling because it is firm and has a distinctive flavor, which is enhanced here by the sweet-tart character of balsamic vinegar. Cod or grouper can be substituted for the swordfish. Serve with a salad of orzo flecked with dried currants.

¼ cup (2 fl oz/60 ml) balsamic vinegar

¾ cup (6 oz/185 g) unsalted butter, at room temperature, cut into small pieces

6 swordfish steaks, each 5–6 oz (155–185 g) and ½ inch (12 mm) thick

olive oil for brushing

salt and ground pepper to taste

Prepare a medium-hot fire for direct-heat cooking in a grill (see page 13). Position the rack 4–6 inches (10–15 cm) from the fire.

In a small saucepan over medium heat, bring the vinegar to a boil and reduce to about 2 tablespoons, about 5 minutes. Remove from the heat and transfer to the top pan of a double boiler or a heatproof bowl placed over (not touching) hot water in a saucepan. Whisk in the butter, a few pieces at a time, until it is fully incorporated. Keep warm until ready to serve.

Brush the fish steaks on both sides with olive oil and season with salt and pepper. Arrange on a grill screen on the grill, and grill until lightly browned, 2–3 minutes. Turn the fish over and continue to grill until it is opaque throughout, 2–3 minutes longer.

Transfer to warmed individual plates and spoon the hot balsamic sauce over the top, dividing evenly. Serve hot. ✱

Flounder with Orange Salsa

SERVES 6

Flounder fillets are thin, so here they are quickly grilled on a bed of orange slices without turning. Serve them with couscous or rice.

FOR THE ORANGE SALSA

3 large oranges

1 small red (Spanish) onion, chopped

2 jalapeño chiles, seeded and chopped

½ cup (¾ oz/20 g) chopped fresh cilantro (fresh coriander)

2 tablespoons orange or lime juice

3 oranges

6 flounder fillets, 5–6 oz (155–185 g) each

vegetable oil or canola oil for brushing

1 bunch fresh chives, trimmed

56

To make the salsa, cut a slice off the top and bottom of each orange to expose the fruit. Place each orange upright on a cutting board and thickly slice off the peel in strips, cutting around the contour of the flesh. Holding the orange over a bowl, cut along either side of each section, letting the sections drop into the bowl. Remove any seeds and discard, then chop the sections and return them to the bowl. Add the onion, chiles, cilantro, and orange or lime juice and toss to mix. Cover and refrigerate until serving. Toss before serving.

Prepare a medium-hot fire for direct-heat cooking in a covered grill (see page 13). Position the rack 4–6 inches (10–15 cm) from the fire.

Peel the remaining 3 oranges in the same way as the oranges were peeled for the salsa, but do not section. Cut crosswise into thin slices. Arrange the orange slices on an oiled grill screen and top with the flounder fillets in a single layer. Brush the fish with oil and set the chives decoratively over the fish.

Put the screen on the grill rack, cover, open the vents, and grill until the fish flakes easily when pierced with a fork, 7–10 minutes. Using a spatula, transfer the fillets, with the orange slices underneath to individual plates. Serve with the salsa. ✳

Lobster Tails with Romesco Sauce

SERVES 6

FOR THE ROMESCO SAUCE

1 ripe tomato, peeled, seeded, and chopped

3 cloves garlic, crushed

3–4 tablespoons (¾–1 oz/20–30 g) ground almonds

¼ teaspoon red pepper flakes

¼ teaspoon salt

¾ cup (6 fl oz/180 ml) olive oil

¼ cup (2 fl oz/60 ml) dry sherry

2 tablespoons red wine vinegar

6 lobster tails, 8–10 oz (250–315 g), thawed if frozen
unsalted butter, melted

To make the sauce, in a food processor or blender, combine the tomato, garlic, almonds, red pepper flakes, and salt. Process until a smooth purée forms. In a small bowl, whisk together the olive oil, sherry, and vinegar. With the motor running, slowly drizzle in the oil mixture, processing until smooth and thick. Taste and adjust the seasonings. Pour into a bowl and set aside. You should have about 1 cup (8 fl oz/250 ml).

Prepare a medium-hot fire for indirect-heat cooking in a covered grill (see page 13). Position the rack 4–6 inches (10–15 cm) from the fire.

Using scissors and working with 1 lobster at a time, split the tail shell open lengthwise. Brush the lobster meat with the butter.

Place the lobster tails on the grill, cut side up. Cover, open the vents, and cook, without turning, until the shells turn red and the meat is opaque throughout, about 10 minutes.

Transfer the lobster tails to warmed individual plates and serve hot. Pass the sauce at the table. ✳

Greek-Style Whole Bass with Olives and Feta

SERVES 6

Grilled fish similar to this recipe are enjoyed in sun-drenched villages throughout Greece. Substitute red snapper or trout for the bass, if you like, and serve with warm pita bread and yogurt flavored with minced garlic.

½ cup (4 fl oz/125 ml) lemon juice

⅓ cup (3 fl oz/80 ml) olive oil

1 tablespoon chopped fresh oregano

3 whole bass, about 1¼ lb (625 g) each, cleaned

leaves from 1 bunch fresh parsley, chopped

1 large yellow onion, chopped

1 cup (5 oz/155 g) Kalamata olives, pitted

½ lb (250 g) feta cheese, crumbled

58

Prepare a medium-hot fire for direct-heat cooking in a covered grill (see page 13). Position the rack 4–6 inches (10–15 cm) from the fire.

In a small bowl, stir together the lemon juice, olive oil, and oregano.

Make 2 diagonal slits on both sides of each fish, cutting into the thickest part. Brush the fish on both sides with the oil mixture. Place on the grill rack, cover, open the vents, and cook, turning once, until the fish are opaque throughout, about 10 minutes.

Just before the fish are ready, divide the parsley and the onion evenly among warmed individual plates. Transfer the fish to the plates, placing them on top of the parsley and onion. Sprinkle the olives and cheese over the fish, dividing evenly. Serve at once. ✳

Grilled Chicken with Sage

SERVES 4–6

½ cup (4 fl oz/125 ml) tangerine or orange juice

¼ cup (2 fl oz/60 ml) olive oil

2 teaspoons peeled and grated fresh ginger

1 chicken, 3½ lb (1.75 kg)

8 fresh sage leaves

3 cloves garlic, crushed

salt and ground pepper to taste

In a large bowl, stir together the tangerine or orange juice, olive oil, and ginger. Add the chicken and turn to coat evenly. Cover and refrigerate for 3 hours.

Prepare a medium-hot fire for indirect-heat cooking in a covered grill (see page 13). Position the rack 4–6 inches (10–15 cm) from the fire.

60

Remove the chicken from the marinade and place on a work surface. Using your fingers and starting at the cavity, carefully loosen the breast skin from the meat. Do not tear the skin. Gently slip the sage leaves under the skin, distributing them evenly. Rub the chicken with the crushed garlic and season with salt and pepper.

Place the chicken, breast side up, on a small piece of aluminum foil (to prevent the bottom of the chicken from burning) on the grill rack. Cover, open the vents, and grill until the juices run clear when a thigh joint is pierced or an instant-read thermometer inserted into the thigh at the thickest part away from the bone registers 180°F (82°C), 50–60 minutes. Add more hot coals to the fire as needed to maintain a constant temperature. Remove the foil for the last 10 minutes of grilling.

Transfer the chicken to a warmed platter, tent with aluminum foil, and let rest for about 10 minutes. Carve at the table and serve hot. ✳

Brined Turkey

SERVES 8

Brining a turkey takes little effort and greatly enhances the juiciness of the meat, but you need to start the process at least 12 hours before the bird goes on the grill. Serve with garlic mashed potatoes and cranberry sauce for a festive holiday meal.

FOR THE BROWN SUGAR BRINE

1 cup (8 oz/250 g) kosher salt

½ cup (3½ oz/105 g) firmly packed dark brown sugar

1 qt (1 l) warm water

3 qt (3 l) cold water

1 turkey, 10–12 lb (5–6 kg)

vegetable oil for rubbing

In a nonaluminum container large enough to hold the turkey and the brine, make the brine: Combine the kosher salt, brown sugar, and warm water, stirring to dissolve the salt and sugar. Add the cold water and stir well.

61

Remove any giblets from the cavity of the turkey and save for another use. Trim off the tail and the wing tips. Rinse the turkey with cold running water, then immerse it in the brine. (If the brine does not cover the turkey completely, mix up an additional half recipe, or as needed, to cover.) Cover the container and refrigerate for at least 12 hours or for up to 24 hours. Drain, rinse with cold running water, and pat dry with paper towels.

Prepare a medium-hot fire for indirect-heat cooking in a covered grill (see page 13). Position the rack 4–6 inches (10–15 cm) from the fire.

Rub the outside of the turkey with vegetable oil. Place the turkey, breast side up, on a small piece of aluminum foil on the grill rack. Cover, partially close the vents, and grill until the juices run clear when a thigh joint is pierced or an instant-read thermometer inserted into the thigh at the thickest part away from the bone registers 180°F (82°C), 3½–4½ hours. Add more hot coals to the fire as needed to maintain a constant temperature and add water to the water pan as necessary. Remove the foil for the last 10 minutes of grilling.

Transfer the turkey to a cutting board and let rest for 10 minutes. Carve into slices and arrange on a platter. Serve hot or warm. ✳

Southwestern Barbecued Chicken

SERVES 6

FOR THE BARBECUE SAUCE

3 slices bacon, cut into ½-inch (12-mm) pieces

¾ cup (3 oz/90 g) chopped yellow onion

2 cloves garlic, minced

1¾ cups (14 fl oz/430 ml) tomato ketchup

¼ cup (2 fl oz/60 ml) pineapple juice

2 tablespoons light corn syrup

1 teaspoon Worcestershire sauce

2 teaspoons chili powder

1 teaspoon ground cumin

¼ teaspoon salt

¼ teaspoon ground pepper

1 chicken, about 3½ lb (1.75 kg), cut into serving pieces

To make the sauce, in a saucepan over medium heat, fry the bacon, stirring occasionally, until crisp, about 5 minutes. Using a slotted spoon, transfer the bacon to paper towels to drain. Add the onion and garlic and sauté over medium heat, stirring occasionally, until tender, about 5 minutes. Add the ketchup, pineapple juice, corn syrup, Worcestershire sauce, chili powder, cumin, salt, and pepper. Bring to a boil, reduce the heat to low, and continue to cook, stirring occasionally, until slightly thickened, 8–10 minutes. Transfer to a bowl and let cool.

Prepare a medium-hot fire for indirect-heat cooking in a covered grill (see page 13). Position the rack 4–6 inches (10–15 cm) from the fire.

Place the chicken pieces on an oiled grill rack, cover, open the vents, and grill, turning the pieces every 15 minutes or so, until the juices run clear when a thigh is pierced, 40–60 minutes. Add more hot coals to the fire if needed to maintain a constant temperature. During the last 15 minutes of grilling, brush the chicken pieces with some of the barbecue sauce.

Transfer to a warmed platter and brush with the remaining sauce. Serve hot. ✳

Pacific Rim Chicken with Peanut Sauce

SERVES 6

Serve the chicken strips over noodles and garnish with chopped fresh cilantro (fresh coriander), bean sprouts, shredded coconut, lime wedges, shredded carrots, and chopped peanuts.

6 boneless, skinless chicken breasts, cut into long strips
1 inch (2.5 cm) wide (12 strips)

1 cup (8 fl oz/250 ml) lime juice

FOR THE PEANUT SAUCE

2 tablespoons vegetable oil

3 green (spring) onions, including tender green tops, chopped

1½ cups (12 fl oz/375 ml) coconut milk, or as needed

½ cup (5 oz/155 g) peanut butter

¼ cup (⅓ oz/10 g) chopped fresh cilantro (fresh coriander)

3 tablespoons dark brown sugar

1½ teaspoons ground ginger

½ teaspoon ground cumin

64

Place the chicken in a shallow nonaluminum dish, pour the lime juice evenly over the top, cover, and refrigerate for 30 minutes.

If using wooden skewers, soak 6 of them in water to cover for 20 minutes, then drain. Meanwhile, prepare a medium-hot fire for direct-heat cooking in a covered grill (see page 13). Position the rack 4–6 inches (10–15 cm) from the fire.

Meanwhile, make the peanut sauce: In a small saucepan over medium heat, warm the vegetable oil. Add the green onions and sauté until tender, about 5 minutes. Stir in the 1½ cups (12 fl oz/375 ml) coconut milk, the peanut butter, cilantro, brown sugar, ginger, and cumin. Cook, stirring occasionally, until the sauce thickens slightly, about 5 minutes. If the sauce becomes too thick to pour, add more coconut milk. Pour into a bowl and let cool. (If made ahead, cover and refrigerate until serving.)

Drain the chicken and weave 2 chicken strips onto each skewer. Place the skewers on the grill rack, cover, open the vents, and grill, turning once, until opaque throughout, about 10 minutes. During the last 5 minutes of grilling, measure out about ¼ cup (2 fl oz/60 ml) of the peanut sauce and brush the chicken lightly with the sauce.

Transfer the skewers to a serving platter and serve hot. Pass the remaining peanut sauce at the table. ✶

Turkey Breast with Ancho Rub

SERVES 6

*Serve the sliced turkey with warm corn bread and mashed
sweet potatoes garnished with dried cranberries.*

FOR THE ANCHO RUB

3 ancho chiles

4 cloves garlic, mashed

2 tablespoons chili powder

2 tablespoons paprika

1 tablespoon grated lemon zest

½ teaspoon ground cinnamon

1 boneless turkey breast, about 1½ lb (750 g)

vegetable oil for brushing

To make the ancho rub, discard the seeds from the chiles, then tear
the chiles into small pieces. Transfer to a spice grinder and grind
into a powder. In a small bowl, combine the ground anchos, the garlic,
chili powder, paprika, lemon zest, and cinnamon.

Brush the turkey breast with the vegetable oil, then spread the chili
mixture evenly over the entire surface. Place in a nonaluminum
dish, cover, and refrigerate for at least 6 hours or for up to 24 hours.

Prepare a medium-hot fire for indirect-heat cooking in a covered
grill (see page 13). Position the rack 4–6 inches (10–15 cm) from
the fire.

Place the turkey breast on the grill rack, cover, partially close the
vents, and grill until an instant-read thermometer inserted into the
thickest part of the breast away from the bone registers 170°F (77°C),
about 1 hour and 20 minutes. Add more hot coals to the fire as
needed to maintain a constant temperature and add water to the
water pan as necessary.

Transfer the turkey breast to a cutting board, tent with aluminum
foil, and let rest for 5–10 minutes. Thinly slice the breast and
arrange on a platter. Serve hot or warm. ✳

Mexican Skirt Steak with Grilled Onions and Peppers

SERVES 6

Slicing the meat against the grain, which runs along the short side of a skirt steak, will make the difference between a tender, flavorful steak and one that is unchewably tough. Serve with tortillas warmed on the grill, guacamole, fresh salsa, and plenty of ice-cold beer.

FOR THE CUMIN MARINADE

1½ cups (12 fl oz/375 ml) lime juice

¼ cup (2 fl oz/60 ml) vegetable oil

2 tablespoons chopped fresh cilantro (fresh coriander)

2 teaspoons ground cumin

2 lb (1 kg) skirt steak

1 large yellow onion, cut into slices ½ inch (12 mm) thick

3 green bell peppers (capsicums), seeded and cut lengthwise into strips ½ inch (12 mm) wide

salt and ground pepper to taste

68

To make the marinade, in a shallow nonaluminum dish, whisk together the lime juice, vegetable oil, cilantro, and cumin. Add the steak and turn to coat evenly. Cover and refrigerate for 4–6 hours.

Prepare a medium-hot fire for direct-heat cooking in a grill (see page 13). Position the rack 4–6 inches (10–15 cm) from the fire.

Remove the steak from the marinade. Pour the marinade into a small saucepan and set over medium-high heat. Bring to a boil, reduce the heat to low, and cook, stirring occasionally, about 5 minutes. Let cool, then brush the onion slices with the marinade.

Place the steaks on the grill rack and grill, turning once, for 5–6 minutes on each side for medium-rare. Put the onion slices and pepper strips on an oiled grill screen and grill until they are browned and tender, 3–5 minutes on each side for the onion slices and 2–3 minutes for the pepper strips.

Transfer the vegetables to a warmed large bowl and the meat to a cutting board. Cut the meat across the grain into thin slices and add to the bowl. Season with salt and pepper and toss well. Serve hot. ✳

69

The Best Backyard Hamburger, Grilled Mushrooms, and Jalapeño Ketchup

SERVES 6

Few meals are more appealing to the entire family than old-fashioned hamburgers topped with mushrooms and served with homemade ketchup. If you don't have time to make the jalapeño-spiked ketchup, look for one at a specialty-food store.

FOR THE JALAPEÑO KETCHUP

2 lb (1 kg) ripe tomatoes

1 yellow onion, minced

¼ cup (2 fl oz/60 ml) cider vinegar

¼ cup (2 oz/60 g) firmly packed dark brown sugar

¼ teaspoon ground cinnamon

¼ teaspoon salt

¼ teaspoon ground pepper

2 jalapeño chiles, seeded and chopped, or to taste

2 lb (1 kg) ground (minced) sirloin, top round, or chuck

1 small yellow onion, chopped

salt and ground pepper to taste

1 lb (500 g) fresh white mushrooms, brushed clean and sliced

vegetable oil for brushing

6 hamburger buns, split

6 leaves fresh lettuce

The day before serving, make the ketchup: In a food processor or blender, working in batches, purée the tomatoes. Pass through a sieve placed over a bowl; discard the contents of the sieve. Transfer to a saucepan and add the onion, vinegar, brown sugar, cinnamon, salt, pepper, and jalapeño chiles. Bring to a boil over medium-high heat, reduce the heat to low, and continue to cook, uncovered, until the mixture reduces to a thick ketchuplike consistency, 20–30 minutes. Remove from the heat, let cool, and pour into a jar. Cover and

(continued on next page)

71

(continued from previous page)

refrigerate until ready to serve. You should have about 1 cup (8 fl oz/ 250 ml); stir well and bring to room temperature before serving.

Prepare a medium-hot fire for direct-heat cooking in a covered grill (see page 13). Position the rack 4–6 inches (10–15 cm) from the fire.

In a bowl, combine the meat with the onion, salt, and pepper. Mix well. Dampen your hands, divide the mixture into 6 equal portions, and shape each portion into a patty about 1 inch (2.5 cm) thick. Brush the mushrooms with vegetable oil and place on an oiled grill screen.

Place the patties and the grill screen on the grill rack and grill, turning once, until the mushrooms are tender and browned and the burgers are done to your liking, about 10 minutes for medium. About 2 minutes before the burgers are ready, place the buns, cut sides down, on the grill rack to toast lightly.

Transfer the buns to individual plates and top each bottom with a lettuce leaf and a burger. Divide the mushrooms evenly among the burgers. Pass the ketchup at the table. Serve hot. ✳

Butterflied Leg of Lamb with Mediterranean Rub

SERVES 6–8

Serve the grilled lamb with grilled garlic, pita bread that has been wrapped in foil and warmed at the edge of the grill, and a Greek salad with tomatoes and feta cheese.

FOR THE MEDITERRANEAN RUB

¼ cup (1½ oz/45 g) dried rosemary

¼ cup (2 oz/60 g) firmly packed dark brown sugar

2 tablespoons dried oregano

4 cloves garlic, minced

salt and ground pepper to taste

1 bone-in leg of lamb, 7–8 lb (3.5–4 kg), boned, butterflied, and trimmed of fat (4½–5 lb/2.25–2.5 kg boned weight)

73

In a food processor or a mortar, combine the rosemary, brown sugar, oregano, garlic, salt, and pepper. Process, or grind with a pestle, until fine. (The rub can be made up to 24 hours in advance and refrigerated in a lock-top plastic bag.) Rub the mixture all over the lamb, pressing it into the meat so that it adheres to the surface. Place in a nonaluminum dish, cover, and refrigerate overnight.

Prepare a medium-hot fire for indirect-heat cooking in a covered grill (see page 13). Position the rack 4–6 inches (10–15 cm) from the fire.

Place the lamb on the grill rack directly over the heat source and sear, turning once, 3–4 minutes on each side. Transfer the lamb to the center of the grill rack, cover, open the vents, and grill, turning once, until an instant-read thermometer inserted into the thickest part registers 140°F (60°C) for medium-rare, about 35 minutes.

Transfer to a cutting board and let rest for 5 minutes. Cut across the grain into thin slices, arrange them on a platter, and serve warm. ✳

Hickory-Smoked Ribs

SERVES 4–6

4 slabs baby back ribs, 4–5 lb (2–2.5 kg) total weight

1½ cups (12 fl oz/375 ml) beer or water

FOR THE GEORGIA MOP SAUCE

¼ cup (2 fl oz/60 ml) vegetable oil

1 yellow onion, minced

2 cloves garlic, minced

1 can (15 oz/470 g) tomato sauce

¼ cup (2 fl oz/60 ml) tomato ketchup

¼ cup (2 fl oz/60 ml) cider vinegar

¼ cup (2 fl oz/60 ml) orange juice

¼ cup (2 oz/60 g) firmly packed dark brown sugar

2 tablespoons Dijon mustard

1 teaspoon Worcestershire sauce

salt and ground pepper to taste

75

Prepare a medium-hot fire for indirect-heat cooking in a covered grill (see page 13). Position the rack 4–6 inches (10–15 cm) from the fire. Soak 3 handfuls of hickory chips in water to cover for at least 20 minutes.

Place each rib rack on a piece of heavy-duty aluminum foil. Sprinkle with 3–4 tablespoons of the beer or water. Wrap tightly and place on the grill rack. Cover, open the vents, and cook for 35 minutes.

Meanwhile, prepare the sauce: In a saucepan over medium heat, warm the oil. Add the onion and garlic and sauté until tender, about 5 minutes. Stir in the tomato sauce, ketchup, vinegar, orange juice, brown sugar, mustard, Worcestershire sauce, salt, and pepper. Bring to a boil, reduce the heat to low, and cook until thick, about 15 minutes.

Sprinkle the hickory chips over the hot coals. Unwrap the ribs, place on the grill rack, cover, partially close the vents, and grill until tender, 20–30 minutes. During the last 10 minutes of grilling, brush the ribs with the sauce. Transfer the ribs to a work surface, cut the racks in half, and mop with more sauce. Pass the remaining sauce at the table. ✴

Slow-Cooked Texas Brisket

SERVES 6

Brisket is a tough cut and needs to cook for a long time over low heat, so be sure to start early in the day. You can extend the life of the fire by using hardwood chips, which burn slowly. Serve the brisket with Corn and Pepper Salsa (page 17), potato salad, and coleslaw.

FOR THE CHILI PASTE

¼ cup (1½ oz/45 g) minced garlic

1 tablespoon ground pepper

1 tablespoon paprika

1 tablespoon chili powder

2 teaspoons minced fresh rosemary

1½ teaspoons ground cumin

⅓ cup (3 fl oz/80 ml) vegetable oil

1 beef brisket, about 4½ lb (2.25 kg)

FOR THE TEXAS SAUCE

3 tablespoons bacon drippings or vegetable oil

1 yellow onion, minced

3 ripe tomatoes, minced, including liquid

1 cup (8 fl oz/250 ml) tomato ketchup

¼ cup (2 oz/60 g) firmly packed dark brown sugar

¼ cup (2 fl oz/60 ml) cider vinegar

1 tablespoon chili powder

1 teaspoon Worcestershire sauce

76

To make the chili paste, in a shallow nonaluminum dish, stir together the garlic, pepper, paprika, chili powder, rosemary, cumin, and vegetable oil. Put the brisket in the dish and rub the entire surface with the paste. Cover and refrigerate overnight. Bring the brisket to room temperature before grilling.

Meanwhile, make the sauce: In a saucepan over medium heat, warm the bacon drippings or vegetable oil. Add the onion and sauté, stirring occasionally, until tender, about 5 minutes. Stir in the tomatoes, ketchup, brown sugar, vinegar, chili powder, and Worcestershire sauce. Simmer, stirring occasionally, until thickened, 10–15 minutes. Taste and adjust the seasonings. Remove from the heat, let cool, cover, and refrigerate until serving.

Prepare a medium-hot fire for indirect-heat cooking in a covered grill (see page 13). Position the rack 4–6 inches (10–15 cm) from the fire. Soak 3 handfuls of hickory chips in water to cover for at least 20 minutes.

Sprinkle the hickory chips over the hot coals, set the brisket on the grill rack directly over the water pan, cover, and grill the brisket, turning once or twice, until it is well browned and very tender, about 1¼ hours per pound (500 g), or a total of 5½ hours. Add more hot coals to the fire every 45 minutes or as needed to maintain a constant temperature, and replace the water in the water pan as needed.

Transfer the brisket to a cutting board and let rest for 5–10 minutes. Reheat the sauce. Cut the brisket across the grain into thin slices. Serve warm with the sauce. ✳

Hoisin Pork Loin

SERVES 6–8

FOR THE SAUCE

1 cup (8 fl oz/250 ml) hoisin sauce

3 tablespoons honey

2 tablespoons dry sherry

1 teaspoon Asian sesame oil

1 boneless pork loin, 3 lb (1.5 kg)

1 lb (500 g) baby bok choy

1 lb (500 g) baby carrots, peeled

vegetable oil for brushing

78

To make the sauce, in a small saucepan over medium heat, combine the hoisin sauce, honey, sherry, and sesame oil. Bring to a boil, stirring constantly. Reduce the heat to low and cook until slightly thickened, 2–3 minutes. Remove from the heat and let cool. Place the pork in a nonaluminum dish and brush it with about one-third of the sauce. Cover and refrigerate for 4–6 hours.

Bring a saucepan three-fourths full of lightly salted water to a boil. Add the bok choy and parboil for 5 minutes. Using a slotted spoon, transfer to a plate. Add the carrots to the same boiling water and parboil for 5 minutes, drain, and set aside with the bok choy.

Prepare a medium-hot fire for indirect-heat cooking in a covered grill (see page 13). Position the rack 4–6 inches (10–15 cm) from the fire.

Place the pork on the grill rack, cover, partially close the vents, and grill, turning once, until an instant-read thermometer inserted into the roast at the thickest part registers 140°F (70°C), 30–45 minutes. About 10 minutes before the pork is done, brush the bok choy and carrots with vegetable oil, place on a grill screen, and grill, turning as necessary, until the vegetables are lightly browned and tender when pierced, 10–15 minutes.

Transfer the pork to a cutting board and let rest for 5 minutes. Remove the vegetables from the screen and keep warm. Slice the pork thinly against the grain and brush with the remaining sauce. Surround with the grilled vegetables and serve hot. ✳

DESSERTS

Pound Cake Kabobs with Chocolate-Coffee Sauce

SERVES 6

FOR THE CHOCOLATE-COFFEE SAUCE

4 oz (125 g) unsweetened chocolate, chopped

¼ cup (2 oz/60 g) unsalted butter

1 cup (8 oz/250 g) sugar

½ cup (4 fl oz/125 ml) evaporated milk

2 tablespoons coffee liqueur

1 teaspoon vanilla extract (essence)

6 slices pound cake, each 1 inch (2.5 cm) thick, cut into 1-inch (2.5-cm) cubes

3 bananas, peeled and cut into 1-inch (2.5-cm) lengths

melted unsalted butter for brushing

whipped cream for garnishing (optional)

To make the sauce, combine the chocolate and butter in the top pan of a double boiler or in a heatproof bowl. Place over (not touching) simmering water in a pan. Stir until smooth.

Using a rubber spatula, scrape the chocolate mixture into a clean saucepan. Stir in the sugar and evaporated milk and bring to a simmer over medium-high heat, stirring until the sugar dissolves and the sauce is heated through. Stir in the liqueur and vanilla and remove from the heat.

Prepare a medium-hot fire for direct-heat cooking in a grill (see page 13). Position the rack 4–6 inches (10–15 cm) from the fire. Soak 6 wooden skewers in water to cover for 30 minutes and drain.

Gently rewarm the sauce on low heat. Thread the cake and banana pieces alternately onto the skewers, dividing them evenly. Brush with the butter and grill, turning once, until the cake is lightly toasted, about 1 minute on each side.

Pour a pool of the warm chocolate sauce onto 6 individual plates, dividing evenly. Add a dollop of whipped cream, if desired. Place one skewer on each plate, drizzle with some of the warmed sauce, and serve hot. ✱

Grilled Brie with Papaya

SERVES 6

Brie's protective coating makes the cheese a natural for the grill. Select a wedge that gives slightly when pressed. If desired, omit the papaya, sprinkle the grilled Brie with slivered blanched almonds, and serve with a large bunch of green grapes and slices of French bread.

1 ripe papaya, about 1 lb (500 g), peeled, halved, seeded, and cut lengthwise into slices ½ inch (12 mm) thick

melted unsalted butter for brushing

1 wedge Brie cheese, ½ lb (250 g)

¼ cup (2 oz/60 g) sugar

Prepare a medium-hot fire for direct-heat cooking in a grill (see page 13). Position the rack 4–6 inches (10–15 cm) from the fire.

Brush the papaya slices with melted butter. Place the papaya slices and the cheese on an oiled grill screen on the grill rack. Grill, turning the papaya and cheese once, for 1–2 minutes on each side for the cheese and 2 minutes on each side for the papaya. The cheese should be warm and just beginning to run and the papaya slices should be warm and soft. Transfer the cheese and papaya slices to a serving platter and sprinkle the papaya with the sugar. Serve warm. ✳

Grilled Rum-Raisin Bananas with Ice Cream

SERVES 6

½ cup (3 oz/90 g) raisins

¼ cup (2 oz/60 g) dark rum, or as needed to cover

½ cup (3½ oz/105 g) firmly packed light brown sugar

6 large, firm but ripe bananas, peeled and halved lengthwise

melted unsalted butter for brushing

1 quart (32 fl oz/1 l) good-quality vanilla ice cream

In a small bowl, combine the raisins with rum to cover. Let stand for about 30 minutes.

Prepare a medium-hot fire for direct-heat cooking in a grill (see page 13). Position the rack 4–6 inches (10–15 cm) from the fire.

Spread the brown sugar on a plate. Brush the bananas with butter and then roll in the sugar. Set the bananas on an oiled grill screen, place on the grill rack, and grill, turning as necessary, until warm and soft and beginning to color, about 2 minutes on each side.

Divide the ice cream evenly among individual bowls or plates, placing 2 scoops in each. Top with the banana halves and sprinkle with the rum-soaked raisins. Serve immediately. ✳

85

Tropical Fruits with Toasted Coconut

SERVES 6

1 cup (4 oz/125 g) shredded or flaked dried coconut

melted unsalted butter for brushing

3 large, ripe mangoes

6 pineapple slices, each ½ inch (12 mm) thick

2 star fruits, cut into slices ¼ inch (6 mm) thick

½ cup (3 oz/90 g) chopped crystallized ginger

Preheat an oven to 325°F (165°C). Spread the coconut on a nonstick baking sheet and toast in the oven, shaking the baking sheet a few times to prevent burning, until lightly browned, about 8 minutes. Set aside.

Prepare a medium-hot fire for direct-heat cooking in a grill (see page 13). Position the rack 4–6 inches (10–15 cm) from the fire.

Working with 1 mango at a time and holding it upright on a cutting board, cut the flesh off the flat sides of the pit in 2 large slabs, cutting as close to the pit as possible. Do not peel. Brush the cut side of each mango slice with melted butter, then brush the pineapple slices and star fruit slices on both sides with melted butter.

Arrange the mango slices, cut sides down, on an oiled grill screen along with the pineapple and star fruit slices. Place on the grill rack and grill, turning the pineapple and star fruit slices once (do not turn the mango slices), until the fruits are warm and soft, 3–4 minutes total. The fruits may brown slightly.

Transfer to a serving dish and sprinkle with the crystallized ginger and toasted coconut. Serve warm. ✳

Pear Bruschetta

SERVES 6

*Sprinkle the pears with chopped pistachios or almonds
just before serving, if desired.*

6 slices brioche or similar dense, rich bread,
each about ½ inch (12 mm) thick

3 large, ripe Bosc pears, peeled, cored, and sliced

melted unsalted butter for brushing

½ cup (5 oz/155 g) raspberry jam

Prepare a medium-hot fire for direct-heat cooking in a covered grill (see page 13). Position the rack 4–6 inches (10–15 cm) from the fire.

Brush the bread slices and the pear slices on both sides with melted butter and arrange on an oiled grill screen. Cover, open the vents, and grill, turning once, until the bread slices are just toasted, about 2 minutes on each side, and the pear slices are warm and soft, 2–3 minutes on each side. Watch the bread closely, as it can char easily.

Transfer the bread slices to a platter and spread the raspberry jam over the tops, dividing evenly. Arrange the pear slices decoratively on the jam. Serve warm. ✳

88

Angel Food Cake with Peaches

SERVES 6

You can make your own angel food cake—white or chocolate is good—or buy one from a bakery. To peel the peaches, dip them in boiling water for about 30 seconds, then lift them out. The skins will slip off easily.

6 slices angel food cake, each about 3 inches (7.5 cm) thick

melted unsalted butter for brushing

4 large peaches, peeled, pitted, and sliced about ½ inch (12 mm) thick

¼ cup (2 oz/60 g) sugar

1 quart (32 fl oz/1 l) peach ice cream

Prepare a medium-hot fire for direct-heat cooking in a grill (see page 13). Position the rack 4–6 inches (10–15 cm) from the fire.

Brush the cake slices lightly on both sides with melted butter. Lightly brush the peach slices with butter and sprinkle them with the sugar.

Arrange the cake slices and peaches on an oiled grill screen and grill, turning the cake once and the peaches as necessary, until the peaches are warm and soft and the cake slices are warm and crusty, about 3 minutes total.

Transfer the cake slices to individual plates and top them with the warm peaches and the ice cream, dividing evenly. Serve warm. ✴

89

Nectarines, Mascarpone, and Pistachios

SERVES 6

A wide variety of fruits take well to grilling: bananas, melon slices, figs, peaches, nectarines, plums, pears, pineapple slices, and more.

6 large, ripe nectarines, halved and pitted

melted unsalted butter for brushing

¾ cup (6 oz/185 g) mascarpone cheese

3 tablespoons sugar

⅓ cup (2 oz/60 g) chopped pistachio nuts,
plus extra for garnish

Prepare a medium-hot fire for direct-heat cooking in a grill (see page 13). Position the rack 4–6 inches (10–15 cm) from the fire.

Brush the nectarine halves with butter and place, cut sides down, on the oiled rack. Grill, turning once, until heated through and just tender but not mushy, about 10 minutes total.

Meanwhile, in a bowl, stir together the cheese, sugar, and the ⅓ cup (2 oz/60 g) pistachios.

Transfer the nectarine halves, cut sides up, to individual bowls, placing 2 halves in each bowl. Spoon the cheese mixture into the hollows, dividing evenly. Serve hot or warm, sprinkled with pistachios. ✱

90

Grilled Fruit Tart

SERVES 6

You can shape the dough into rectangles, if you like, or make individual tartlets. Grilling time will vary, however, so bake until the pastry is firm to the touch and golden brown on the bottom. Serve the tart with sweetened whipped cream.

1 teaspoon plus 3 tablespoons sugar

scant 1 cup (8 fl oz/250 ml) warm water

1 package (2½ teaspoons) active dry yeast

2¾ cups (14 oz/440 g) all-purpose (plain) flour

½ teaspoon salt

2 tablespoons unsalted butter, at room temperature

1 cup (8 oz/250 g) mascarpone cheese

⅓ cup (2½ oz/75 g) firmly packed light brown sugar

6 cups (1½ lb/750 g) strawberries, stems removed, and halved if large

2 cups (8 oz/250 g) blueberries

1 cup (10 oz/315 g) strawberry jam

¼ cup (2 fl oz/60 ml) water

In a small bowl, stir the 1 teaspoon sugar into the warm water. Sprinkle the yeast over the top and let stand until foamy, about 5 minutes.

In a food processor, combine the flour, the 3 tablespoons sugar, and the salt and pulse briefly to combine. Add the butter and the yeast mixture and process until a soft, slightly sticky dough forms, about 10 seconds.

Turn out the dough onto a lightly floured work surface and knead until smooth, about 5 minutes. If the dough is too sticky, work in additional flour, a tablespoon at a time, until smooth. Gather the dough into a ball, place in a bowl, cover the bowl tightly with buttered plastic wrap, and let the dough rise in a warm place until doubled in bulk, 45–60 minutes.

Punch down the dough and let stand for 5 minutes. Turn out onto the floured work surface and knead for a few minutes until smooth. Stretch and pat the dough into a round about 12 inches (30 cm) in diameter.

Prepare a medium-hot fire for direct-heat cooking in a covered grill (see page 13). Position the rack 4–6 inches (10–15 cm) from the fire. Place a pizza stone on the grill rack.

In a small bowl, stir together the mascarpone cheese and the brown sugar. Spread the cheese mixture over the dough, then the strawberries, and finally the blueberries. In a small saucepan over medium heat, combine the jam and water and stir until melted. Brush the jam mixture over the berries.

Place the tart directly on the hot pizza stone. Cover, open the vents, and grill, rotating the tart 180 degrees after about 5 minutes, until the crust is golden, 8–10 minutes. (This may take longer on a gas grill.)

Transfer to a serving plate, cut into wedges, and serve warm. ✶

93

INDEX